KINSHIP CARE:
A NATURAL BRIDGE

A Report of the
Child Welfare League of America
Based on the Recommendations of the
CWLA North American Kinship Care
Policy and Practice Committee

Child Welfare League of America
Washington, DC

© 1994 by the Child Welfare League of America, Inc.

CHILD WELFARE LEAGUE OF AMERICA, INC.
440 First Street, NW, Suite 310, Washington, DC 20001-2085

CURRENT PRINTING (last digit)
10 9 8 7 6 5 4 3 2 1

Cover design by S. Dmitri Lipczenko
Text design by Eve Malakoff-Klein

Printed in the United States of America

ISBN # 0-87868-584-7

CONTENTS

Preface   v

Introduction   1

Section III: A Framework for the Future

Section IV: Next Steps

Appendices

PREFACE

The Child Welfare League of America (CWLA) has a long tradition of addressing emerging issues in the field of child welfare. As the need has arisen, it has convened commissions, task forces, and work groups—with broad representation from the public and voluntary child welfare sectors—to study a range of child welfare issues, including adoption, family foster care, group residential care, chemical dependency, HIV infection and children, cultural competence in child welfare practice, and child day care. This report represents CWLA's response to another emerging issue—kinship care.

Over the past several years, kinship care has become an increasingly important child welfare service. As the number of children cared for by kin has continued to rise, CWLA member agencies and the child welfare field as a whole have sought policy, program, and practice guidance to help in developing and implementing effective kinship care policies and programs. In response, CWLA initiated a process to develop policy and practice recommendations to assist the field. In 1992, CWLA convened the North American Kinship Care Policy and Practice Committee. Through a series of meetings, the Committee, ably and tirelessly chaired by Ivory Johnson, Deputy Director, San Diego County Department of

Social Services, provided CWLA with public and voluntary child welfare sector expertise on the critical issues involved in kinship care. The work of the Committee formed the basis of this report. CWLA is grateful for the invaluable support and guidance of Ivory Johnson and the Committee, without which this report would not have been possible.

CWLA also expresses its gratitude to the CWLA staff members who gave of themselves above and beyond the call of duty to produce this outstanding report: Dana Burdnell Wilson, Director of Kinship Care; Eileen Mayers Pasztor, Director of Family Foster Care; Pamela Day, Director of Family Preservation and Family Support; Madelyn DeWoody, Director of Child Welfare Services; Eve Malakoff-Klein, Managing Editor; and Nickola Dixon and Sussan Tahmasebi, Program Assistants.

This report provides a series of recommendations and action steps to guide kinship care policy and practice and ensure that children in kinship care, their birth parents, and their kinship parents receive the support and services they need. CWLA is committed to advancing the agenda set forth in this report. We invite other national organizations, the U.S. Department of Health and Human Services, and our member agencies in the public and nonprofit child welfare community to join us in these efforts.

David S. Liederman
Executive Director
Child Welfare League of America

Introduction

> *"The family is at once the most sensitive, important, and enduring element in the culture of any people. Whatever its structure, its most important function is everywhere the same—namely, to insure the survival of its people."*
>
> —Andrew Billingsly
> Sociologist, Author, Professor

The practice of relatives or kin parenting children when their parents cannot is a time-honored tradition in most cultures. In North America, the full time care of children by kin is prevalent in many communities and is increasing substantially in others. Care of children by kin is strongly tied to family preservation. Family strengths often include a kinship network that functions as a support system. The kinship support system may be composed of nuclear family, extended family, blended family, foster family, or adoptive family members, or members of tribes or clans. The involvement of kin may stabilize family situations, ensure the protection of children, and prevent the need to separate children from their families and place them in the formal child welfare system.

Increasingly, however, kinship care is an arrangement that operates within the formal child welfare system. More and more often, when children are separated from their parents as a result of abuse or neglect and are placed in the custody of child welfare agencies, kinship homes are being formally used as placements for children. The phenomenon of placing children with kin for full-time protection, nurturing, and care has prompted child welfare agencies to take a new look at the nature of kinship care, the role of kinship care as a child welfare service, and the relationships among kinship care, family preservation, and out-of-home care. The extent to which federal and state requirements and other standards that generally apply when children are in the legal custody of child welfare agencies apply in the context of kinship care is also is under examination.

Definitions

Because kinship care encompasses many types of caregiving, a broad definition of it is essential. Kinship care may be defined as the full-time nurturing and protection of children who must be separated from their parents by relatives, members of their tribes or clans, godparents, stepparents, or other adults who have a kinship bond with a child. Kinship care arrangements vary. While they always involve caregiving by kin, the arrangements themselves may be made between and among family members or, alternatively, may involve child welfare agencies.

Kinship care is typically categorized in one of two ways: informal and formal. The parenting of children by kin may occur in the context of an informal family arrangement when the family decides the child will live with relatives or other kin. In this arrangements (referred to as informal kinship care in this report), a social worker may be involved in helping family members plan for the child, but a child welfare agency does not assume legal custody of or responsibility for the child.

Even in these informal kinship arrangements, however, children and caregivers may need a range of child welfare services . Some of these services are unique to kinship care. For example, kinship parents may need help in obtaining a legally recognized status, such as temporary custody or guardianship, in order to obtain necessary emergency medical care or prevent the sudden retrieval of the child by a parent who cannot safely care for the child. Kin also may need services such as day care or assistance in meeting the child's health care needs. Because the care of children may drain the emotional and financial resources of kin, self-help groups such as GAP (Grandparents as Parents), ROC (Raising Others' Children), ROCKING (Raising Our Children's Kids, an Intergenerational Network of Grandparents), Grandparents United for Children's Rights, and Second-Time Around Parents have been organized to provide essential supports.

Parents and their relatives are free to arrange informal kinship care when issues relating to the safety and protection of children have not been brought to the attention of the child welfare system. Because the parents have custody of the child, relatives need not be approved, licensed, or supervised by the state. These arrangements are not considered foster care placements, however, and children generally are not eligible to receive the services or financial benefits available to their peers in foster care. Children in such informal arrangements may, however, be able to receive benefits through the Aid to Families with Dependent Children (AFDC) program, which provides financial support at a level usually substantially less than foster care payments. They may also be eligible for financial assistance through child support payments or through benefits available through the Supplemental Security Income (SSI) program. In terms of services, child welfare agencies may provide a range of supports to kin to assist in stabilizing and maintaining families, services that may prevent the need for later court or formal child welfare system involvement.

In contrast to informal kinship care arrangements, formal kinship care involves the parenting of children by kin as a result of a determination by the court and the public child protective service agency that a child must be separated from his or her parents because of abuse, neglect, dependency, abandonment, or special medical circumstances. In formal kinship care, the court places the child in the legal custody of the child welfare agency, and kin provide the full-time care, protection, and nurturing that the child needs. Formal kinship parent status is linked to state and federal child welfare laws that provide for the care of a child in an approved or licensed home. In formal kinship care, children may receive financial assistance through foster care payments, and in turn, kin are expected to meet approval or licensing requirements and to cooperate with the child protection agency in developing and implementing a case plan for the child.

Formal kinship care, as a service within the child welfare system, is the principal focus of this report. While many issues remain regarding the nature of kinship care and its primary role as a family preservation service or as an alternative to family foster care, formal kinship care in its current context is tied inextricably to foster care. As a result, it will be considered in that context in this report.

The Importance of Kinship Care

The incidence of formal kinship care arrangements has grown dramatically in recent years. Increasing numbers of parents are unable to rear their own children because of substance abuse, HIV/AIDS, physical and mental illness, homelessness, and poverty. The number of reports of child abuse and neglect has increased dramatically and consequently, the number of children needing out-of-home care has nearly doubled since 1986. In response to these trends, child welfare agencies increasingly have turned to kin as caregivers for children entering the legal custody of the state.

According to the U.S. Bureau of the Census, approximately 4.3 million children lived with relatives in 1992 [U.S. Bureau of the Census 1992]. While most of these children lived with their mothers in the homes of relatives, some 878,000 lived apart from their parents in their grandparents' homes [U.S. Bureau of the Census 1992]. This number does not include children who live with other kin, a group that is also increasing.

The phenomenon of formal kinship care, however, has caught many child welfare agencies off guard, with no substantive knowledge base or policy, program, and practice guidelines to assist them in developing and implementing quality kinship care programs. As a result, a host of policy and practice issues have arisen that demand attention and resolution. These issues include determining the appropriate level of financial support for children placed with kin; providing services for children, kinship parents, and birth parents; assessing, monitoring and supervising kinship homes; planning for permanency for children in kinship care; and designing and delivering kinship programs. State policies and practice vary widely, and child welfare agencies in the public and voluntary sectors are struggling to define kinship care and clarify its role as a child welfare service; develop appropriate kinship care policies; and institute program and practice guidelines to maximize the appropriate use of kinship care as a resource for children.

Using This Report

This report focuses on formal kinship care. Section I describes the essential place of kinship care in the array of child welfare services, both in terms of family preservation and out-of-home care. It examines the use of kinship care as a child welfare service under P.L. 96-272 and as a support for principles of child-centered, family-focused practice. The growth and characteristics of formal kinship care practice are also examined.

Section II focuses on kinship care policy and practice. In chapter 3, existing policy and law at the federal and state levels, and in relation to litigation, are summarized. Chapter 4, in turn, raises a number of critical policy and practice questions that must be addressed as kinship care policy and practice continue to develop.

In Section III, Chapters 5 and 6 provide a foundation for the future of kinship care by defining guiding principles, then setting forth a policy and practice framework based on those principles. Each component of the framework is described and recommendations and action steps are outlined.

Finally, Section IV provides an action agenda that will support the continuing development and implementation of quality kinship care policy and practice. The agenda addresses needed activities on the part of child welfare agencies, legislative directions, and issues for further research.

❧ Section I ❧
KINSHIP CARE AS A
CHILD WELFARE SERVICE

"Mention the topic of kinship care in a room full of child welfare specialists, and the reactions received will be as numerous and varied as the people in the room."
—Task Force on Permanency Planning [1990]

❧ 1 ❧
The Place of Kinship Care in the Array of Child Welfare Services

Kinship care plays an essential role in the array of child welfare service options. When children cannot be reared safely by their parents, kinship care provides an opportunity to protect children and meet their needs separate from their parents yet with their families. Kinship care often is informally arranged by family without any involvement of child welfare agencies. In this context, kinship care may be a means of preserving family relationships and protecting children without the involvement of the judicial system.

Kinship care also may be an option for formal placement of children with kin by child welfare agencies. Based on the needs of the child, kinship care should be the first option assessed when a child must be separated from his or her parents. However, it is not always a realistic option. Kin may not be available or may be unable to meet the safety and developmental needs of the child. In such cases, other out-of-home care options—such as family foster care or group residential care—must be considered.

Kinship Care as a Family Preservation Service

Kinship care is an important component of family preservation efforts because it can effectively prevent the need for court intervention based on child protection concerns and avoid the formal placement of children in the child welfare system. Intensive family preservation programs and family support programs have a history of enlisting kin to care for children when families are in crisis, and kin traditionally have provided such care for short periods of time, as respite for birth parents, and on an ongoing basis to maintain the child safely within the family. This type of kinship care is most appropriate when there are indicators that parents soon will be able to effectively parent and that formal placement in the child welfare system will be unnecessary.

When kin are able and willing to care for a child, child welfare agencies have an opportunity to strengthen and support families through kinship care. Kinship care services should help families build capacity; promote family functioning, family self-reliance, and the competence of both birth parents and kinship parents; and provide preventive and rehabilitative services to strengthen family ties and enhance the family's coping capacity.

Kinship Care as an Out-of-Home Care Service

Kinship care as a form of out-of-home care involves the legal placement with kin of children who have entered the custody of the state child protection agency because of abuse, neglect, or abandonment. As a form of out-of-home care, kinship care resembles care by foster parents because children are in need of a placement away from their parents. Foster care payments may be provided, and kin may be subject to the same state approval/licensing requirements as unrelated foster parents, including a favorable home study, training or other formal preparation, participation in case planning and implementation of case plans including visits with parents, and adherence to the agency's discipline policy.

Kinship care, however, differs significantly from family foster care because in kinship care established relationships already exist among the child, the parents of the child, and the kinship parents. Family dynamics will affect the relationships among members of the birth and kinship family and the casework staff. These family dynamics can influence the way in which the agency engages in case planning, the development of a helping relationship with the family, permanency planning, reunification of the child with the parent, and pursuit of other permanency options such as adoption or guardianship.

Kinship Care under P.L. 96-272

The Adoption Assistance and Child Welfare Act of 1980 (P.L. 96-272), the primary federal law concerning children and families in the child welfare system, provides a legal basis for defining kinship care as a child welfare issue. The Act requires that when children are separated from their parents and placed in the custody of a public child welfare agency, the state must place them in the "least restrictive alternative available." Although P.L. 96-272 does not expressly mention relatives, the statutory requirement of least restrictive alternative has been interpreted by many child welfare practitioners as a preference for placement with relatives when separation from parents must occur. Some states have enacted child protection statutes that specifically state a preference for placing children with kin. Others include a preference for relative placement in agency policy manuals.

In June 1987, the federal Administration for Children, Youth and Families issued Policy Announcement ACYF-PA-8702 to clarify the requirements of P.L. 96-272 with regard to placement with relatives. The Announcement states that foster care arrangements under P.L. 96-272 include "family foster homes, group homes, and child care institutions, as well as pre-adoptive homes and *relative foster homes*, regardless of whether foster care payments are made by the State and local agency" ... "[T]he circumstances of placement...or the existence of a blood relationship between the foster parent and the child will not be reasons for excluding affected children from the [protections and requirements of P.L. 96-272]" [Policy Announcement ACYF-PA-8702, italics added].

Kinship Care and Child-Centered, Family-Focused Practice

When appropriately assessed, planned for, and supported, kinship care is a child welfare service that reflects the principles of child-centered, family-focused casework practice, the model of practice that child welfare practitioners advocate as the unifying theme for child welfare services.

This model of practice has two critical and related elements: child-centeredness and a family focus. In a child-centered, family-focused system, the child's need for safety, nurturance, and family continuity drive service delivery and funding. Children's needs are considered first, but always in the context of having a family, and always with a focus on maintaining and building family ties. Child-centered, family-focused practice requires that workers, supervisors, and the child welfare system as a whole do two things at once: attend to the child's safety and well-being and work with the family to build the strongest possible caring environment for the child—at home with parents, with kin, with adoptive parents, in planned long-term family foster care, or in other care settings that provide a strong family connection.

A child-centered, family-focused system respects family strengths and diversity, builds upon family resources, views the family as a cohesive and successful unit whenever possible, and works to strengthen families and prevent the unnecessary separation of children from their families. Such a system recognizes that children need families and that it is in families that children thrive, are loved and educated, and are taught family and societal values. Family members are viewed as collaborative partners in service delivery, and interventions are offered to strengthen the ability of the family to care for children and achieve family connectedness. A child-centered, family-focused child welfare system responds to the culturally and ethnically diverse children and families it serves, and is diligent in identifying and eliminating barriers to culturally competent services.

Kinship care can meet the safety, nurturance, and family continuity needs of children and strengthen and support families by:

- Enabling children to live with persons whom they know and trust;

- Reducing the trauma children may experience when they are placed with persons who initially are unknown to them;

- Reinforcing children's sense of identity and self-esteem, which flows from knowing their family history and culture;

- Facilitating children's connections to their siblings;

- Encouraging families to consider and rely on their own family members as resources;

- Enhancing children's opportunities to stay connected to their own communities and promoting community responsibility for children and families; and

- Strengthening the ability of families to give children the support they need.

❧2❧
FORMAL KINSHIP CARE

The Growth in Formal Kinship Care

Formal kinship care has grown dramatically as a child welfare service. A number of factors have affected its development and growth: the increasing number of children in out-of-home care, greater agency recognition of kin as resources for children, the declining number of foster families, and the apparent relationship between kinship care, length of time children stay in care, and enhanced placement stability.

Increasing Numbers of Children in Out-of-Home Care

Child abuse and neglect reports have increased by 100% over the past ten years. In 1992, there were over 2.9 million reports of child abuse and neglect [National Committee for the Prevention of Child Abuse 1993]. At the same time, the number of children needing a range of services, including out-of-home care, significantly increased. By the end of 1992, 442,000 children were in care, up from 276,000 in 1985 [American Public Welfare Association 1993]. The population of children in care is expected to exceed 500,000 by 1995.

As the overall population of children in out-of-home care has increased, so too has the use of kinship care. Urban communities in particular have witnessed dramatic increases in their out-of-home care populations. Substance abuse (and the advent of crack cocaine in particular), poverty, HIV infection, and homelessness have brought increasing numbers of children into the child welfare system who are in need of care outside of their homes. [Congressional Research Service 1993: 10; Testa 1992: 30]. Much of the growth has been in formal kinship care [HHS Inspector General 1992].

The number of children in formal kinship care has risen most dramatically in Illinois, New York, California, and Maryland. Wulczyn and Goerge, in their study on caseload growth in out-of-home care, found that the number of children in New York City's kinship care programs increased from 1,000 in 1986 to 24,000 in 1992. By 1992, kinship care accounted for nearly one-half of the city's children in out-of-home care [Wulczyn and Goerge 1991: 11].

In Illinois, 46 percent (8,387 of 18,125) of the children placed in out-of-home care in 1992 were placed in kinship care. The number of children has increased by more than 200 children per month since August 1990 [State of Illinois, Home of Relative License Report 1992]. In California, two-thirds of the growth in out-of-home care from 1984 to 1989 has been attributed to the dramatic rise in kinship care [Berrick et al. 1991]. Maryland likewise has experienced significant increases in kinship care. In 1986, there were approximately 154 children in kinship care, and almost 3,200 children in foster care with unrelated caregivers. By 1993, the number of children in unrelated foster care had stabilized, but the number of children in kinship care had grown to over 2,800 [Maryland Department of Human Resources 1993]. Reports from the field suggest that the protective placement of children with kin is a trend occurring throughout the country, although exact numbers are difficult to obtain.

Agency Recognition of Kin as Resources for Children

The use of kinship care has increased in part because of the willingness of kin to care for their relative children and agency recognition of kin as resources. In a study by the National Black Child Development Institute in 1986, researchers found that when agencies considered relatives as a resource for children needing out-of-home care, more than half of the relatives contacted offered to assist the child, usually as the child's caregiver [National Black Child Development Institute 1991: 26–29]. Similarly, a study conducted at the University of California at Berkeley of 246 kinship parents and 354 unrelated foster families found that relatives often come forward to care for their kin children either voluntarily or when asked by an agency if they would care for the child [Berrick et al. 1991: 7]. As public child welfare agencies turn to kin as placement resources, relatives are readily responding and providing care.

Declining Number of Foster Families

The increase in kinship care also is attributed to a shortage of non-related foster families. The National Foster Parent Association (NFPA) reported that, between 1985 and 1990, the number of foster families decline by 27 percent while the number of children in out-of-home care increased by 47 percent [National Foster Parent Association 1991]. NFPA estimates that each year, 29 percent of all foster families leave the program [National Foster Parent Association 1991]. As the number of foster families has decreased, child welfare agencies have turned increasingly to kin as resources for children in care.

Length of Stay in Care and Stability of Placement

Research suggests that not only are children entering kinship care in larger numbers than ever before, but that they are remaining in care for longer periods of time than children placed with nonrelated foster parents. A study of children entering care in New York City in 1988 found that 88 percent of those who entered kinship care were still in care in June 1990, compared to 50 percent of those who entered family foster care [Wulczyn and Goerge 1991: 11]. Similar patterns were found in California and Maryland [Benedict and White 1991; Berrick et al. 1991].

Research also suggests that kinship care can provide a stable family arrangement for many children. Children in kinship care are less likely to experience multiple placements than their counterparts in family foster care. Of the children who entered California's foster care system in 1988, for example, only about 23 percent of those placed initially with kin experienced another placement, while 58 percent of children living with unrelated foster families experienced at least one subsequent placement during the following 3.5 years [Berrick et al. 1991].

These findings on length of stay and placement stability have important implications in relation to the increasing numbers of children in out-of-home care in general and in kinship care in particular. The growth in the number of children in out-of-home care is associated with the increased length of stay in kinship care, an issue that impacts on permanency planning. The observed relationship between kinship care and placement stability, however, suggests positive developmental benefits for children cared for by kin.

The Children and Caregivers
in Formal Kinship Care

Research about kinship care is limited and studies primarily have focused on specific communities and, in some cases, involved small samples. Even this limited research, however, provides important information about children in kinship care and the kin who care for them.

Characteristics of Children in Kinship Care

The characteristics and needs of children placed with kin are similar to those of children living with unrelated foster families. One important difference, however, is in the ethnic minority status of children placed with kin.

A 1989 study of 524 children in kinship care in Baltimore, Maryland, found that 90 percent were African American and 10 percent were Caucasian [Dubowitz 1990]. The researchers compared this finding with a 1986 Baltimore study of children placed with nonrelated foster parents and found that children in kinship care were more likely to be African American than children placed with nonrelated foster parents. Likewise, the Berkeley study of 600 kinship and nonrelated caregivers found that, of the children in kinship care, 46 percent were African American (as compared with 28 percent of the children in foster care); 32 percent were Caucasian (as compared with 36 percent in foster care); 14 percent were Latino (as compared with 22 percent in foster care); and 9 percent were from other ethnic groups (as compared with 14 percent in foster care) [Berrick et al. 1991].

Aside from the ethnic minority differences, however, children in kinship care are very similar to children placed with unrelated foster parents in terms of their health and educational needs. The Berkeley study compared children in kinship care and children in nonrelated foster care and found strong similarities between the two groups in terms of health and educational status. In each group, about 15 percent of the children were in fair or poor health; more than 40 percent had been prenatally exposed to drugs; and about 10 percent exhibited fetal alcohol syndrome. The educational status of the children in both groups also was comparable, although children in kinship care were doing somewhat better. Thirty-one percent of children in nonrelated foster care had repeated at least one grade as compared with 23 percent of the children in kinship care, and 32 percent of the children in nonrelated foster care were in special education as compared with 26 percent of the children in kinship care [Berrick et al. 1991].

The Baltimore research also found physical and mental health problems among children in kinship care. Forty-one percent of the children who were living with relatives and enrolled in school were behind at least one grade level and 28 percent were receiving special education services. The children, as a group, tended to test low on achievement tests and to have cognitive and language difficulties. A significant number of the children also exhibited behavioral problems. Although the researchers did not directly compare the health and education status of children in kinship care and in nonrelated foster care, their review of the literature caused them to conclude that the health and educational status of both groups was similar and that the condition of all children in care, whether in kinship care or family foster care, was of concern [Dubowitz 1990].

Characteristics of Kinship Parents

Several studies have focused on the demographic characteristics of kinship parents. Although the results have varied, certain trends among kinship parents can be identified.

1. Most kinship parents are grandmothers or other close relatives. The Baltimore study found that the vast majority of relatives who cared for the 524 kinship children on which the study focused were close relatives: about half were grandmothers; almost one-third were aunts; the remaining caregivers primarily were older siblings, uncles, or grandfathers [Dubowitz 1990]. Similarly, a New York City study of 95 kinship caregivers found that 60 percent were grandmothers and 30 percent were aunts [Thorton 1991: 593–601].

2. Kinship families are predominantly people of color. Ninety percent of the kinship providers that researchers interviewed for the New York City study were African American [Thorton 1991]. In the Berkeley study, 43 percent of the kinship parents were African American (as compared with 22 percent for foster parents), 34 percent were Caucasian (as compared with 63 percent for foster parents), 17 percent were Latino (as compared with 9 percent for foster parents), and 6 percent were from other ethnic groups (as compared to 6 percent for foster parents) [Berrick et al. 1991]. The Baltimore study found that 90 percent of the kinship families were African American and 10 percent were Caucasian [Dubowitz 1990].

3. Kinship parents tend to have limited incomes. In the Berkeley study, kinship parents tended to have lower incomes than unrelated foster parents. When foster care payments were taken into account, the average annual gross income for kin was $32,424; for unrelated foster parents, it was $51,320. When foster care payments were excluded, kin had an average gross income of $21,843, compared to $36,401 for foster parents. Kinship parents were more likely to receive Aid to Families with Dependent Children (AFDC) benefits (33 percent as compared with 6 percent for foster parents) and Social Security benefits (25 percent as compared with 17 percent for foster parents) [Berrick et al. 1991]. In the

New York City study, researchers found that while 41 percent of the kinship caregivers were employed full-time, they were also more likely to receive AFDC benefits (33 percent as compared with 6 percent for foster parents) and Social Security benefits (25 percent as compared with 17 percent for foster parents) [Thorton 1991].

4. *Kinship parents tend to have less formal education than unrelated foster parents.* The Berkeley study found that female kin parents who were interviewed were less likely to have graduated from high school (26 percent had not graduated) than female foster parents (10 percent had not graduated) [Berrick et al. 1991]. In the Baltimore study, less than half of the kinship parents had finished high school, but 19 percent had attended some college [Dubowitz 1990].

❧ Section II ❧
CURRENT POLICY AND PRACTICE

"Kinship care has great potential for bridging gaps between child welfare services and the child's family system, culture, and community."

—James Gleason
Researcher, University of Illinois

❧3❧

EXISTING POLICY AND LAW

Current kinship care policy and practice is shaped by federal policy, state policy and practice, and the results of litigation against child welfare agencies.

Federal Policy

Title IV-B and Title IV-E of the Social Security Act

The principal sources of federal child welfare policy are Title IV-B and Title IV-E of the Social Security Act (P.L. 96-272) and their subsequent amendment by the Omnibus Budget Reconciliation Act (OBRA) of 1993 (P.L. 103-66). Both Title IV-B and Title IV-E have important implications for kinship care.

Title IV-B, which provides federal funding to states for child welfare services, gives states broad discretion in developing and delivering services and requires that certain protections be in place for all children in out-of-home care. The Omnibus Budget Reconciliation Act of 1993 (P.L. 103-66) added a new subpart to Title IV-B that provides states with federal funding for family preservation and family support services. Extended family members are also eligible for the services supported through Title IV-B, including community-based family support services, respite care, services to enhance parenting skills, and in-home services.

Title IV-E provides federal funding to states for foster care maintenance and related administrative, training, and placement costs. An open-ended entitlement, federal Title IV-E funding is available when:

- the child is separated from the parent by a judicial determination that such separation is in the child's best interest or under a voluntary placement agreement that meets federal conditions and restrictions;

- the child's birth family is eligible for Aid to Families with Dependent Children (AFDC);

- the child is physically "removed from the home";

- the placement and care of the child is the responsibility of the state or county child protection agency; and

- the child is placed in a family home or child care institution approved or licensed by the state.

In 1991, approximately 47 percent of the children in out-of-home care were eligible for federal support under Title IV-E [Congressional Research Service 1993]. State and local funds support children in care who are not eligible for Title IV-E benefits.

Title IV-E does not explicitly reference kinship care in relation to placement of children. Certain of its provisions, however, have been interpreted by some states as favoring placement of children with kin: the requirement that "reasonable efforts" be made to prevent the unnecessary separation of children from their families and the mandate that children be placed in the "least restrictive (most family-like) setting available and in close proximity to the parents' home, consistent with the best interest and special needs of the child" [42 U.S.C. 675].

Title IV-E states that federal foster care maintenance payments may be made when children are cared for in a "foster family home" and broadly defines the term as a home for children that either is licensed by the state or has been approved by the state agency having responsibility for licensing homes. Because "foster family home" is broadly defined, federal foster care payments may be made on behalf of children in kinship care provided that the children are Title IV-E eligible and that the state approves or licenses kin as meeting the relevant standards.

Aid to Families with Dependent Children

Title IV-A of the Social Security Act, which establishes the Aid to Families with Dependent Children (AFDC) program, provides federal funding to states for needy children and their caregivers. Recognizing that children often live with kin, the law expressly states that the program is designed to "encourage the care of dependent children in their own homes *or in the homes of relatives* by enabling each state to furnish...assistance...to needy dependent children and the parents and *relatives with whom they are living*" [42 U.S.C. 601, italics added]. AFDC benefits support eligible children and, in cases where kin themselves have low incomes, "the needs of the relative with whom any dependent child is living" [42 U.S.C. 606].

AFDC benefits vary widely among states. On average, they tend to be 50 percent lower than the level of foster care maintenance payments [U.S. House of Representatives Committee on Ways and Means 1993].

State Policy and Practice

As reflected by the kinship care survey conducted in 1992 by the Office of Inspector General, U.S. Department of Health and Human Services, state policies governing kinship care vary widely [HHS Inspector General 1992]. The Inspector General found variation in state policies regarding the following:

1. Expressed preference for kin as caregivers for children in out-of-home care. The report found that the policy of 29 states required preference for placement with relatives; 20 states routinely or occasionally used relatives but did not mandate a preference; and two states discouraged but did not prohibit the use of relatives.

2. *Approval / licensing of kin.* States also varied widely in the process they used to authorize the home of kin for placement of children, and referred to the process as "licensing," "approving" or "certifying." Most states reported some licensing procedure, but varied as to whether they required strict compliance with standards, allowed waivers for kin, or set separate standards for kin. The types of permissible waivers also varied. Most often waived were requirements related to orientation and training for caregivers; caregiver age, martial status, and income; and physical space. Of the 40 states that were able to report the percentage of kinship care homes that they licensed, about half said that they licensed most or all kinship care homes; the remainder said that very few homes were licensed.

3. *Supervision and monitoring of kinship care homes.* Several states reported that their policies for caseworker supervision of kinship care homes were different than that for family foster homes. Generally, fewer home visits were required.

4. *Financial support.* Most states reported that foster care maintenance payments were made for children in kinship care only when kin were approved or licensed. Several states restricted foster care payments, providing them only to kin who were licensed and were caring for children who were eligible for federal Title IV-E benefits. Children in kinship care who did not receive foster care payments often received AFDC benefits if they were eligible for AFDC and the relationship between the child and the caregiver was within the AFDC eligibility guidelines.

5. *Permanency planning.* All states reported policies supporting adoption of children by kin. Financial support in all states was limited, however, to adoptions of children meeting "special needs" criteria. Most states also reported that kin could become guardians for their children, albeit with no financial support. Most states also allowed some form of long-term care by kin, under which foster care payments for eligible children were continued.

Litigation

Several lawsuits have focused on kinship care, particularly on issues related to equity for children and the kin who care for them. The table on the following pages provides the case history and court decision in five significant cases in this area. Three of these cases involve rulings on payment policies for kinship caregivers; two cases focus on the access of children and kin to services.

Briefly, court decisions in the following cases have shaped the existing policy and legal framework for kinship care:

- *Miller v. Youakim.* In the leading kinship care case, the United States Supreme Court ruled that states cannot discriminate against kinship caregivers under the federal foster care program.

- *Lipscomb v. Simmons.* In this case, the court held that Oregon could provide foster care payments to unrelated foster parents and deny state-financed foster care payments to kin.

- *King v. McMahon.* In this case, the court ruled that California could deny state-financed foster care payments to children in kinship care.

- *Eugene F. v. Gross.* Not yet decided by the court, this case nevertheless has prompted New York City to provide a range of financial benefits and services for kin who care for children in the child welfare system similar to those provided to foster parents.

- *L.J. v. Massinga.* In this case, the court required Maryland to assure that children in kinship care have access to specialized services that were previously only available to children in foster care.

❧Table❧

Case	Case History	Court's Final Holding
Miller v. Youakim 440 U.S. 125 (1979)	• **1974:** Case filed in federal district court in Illinois challenging the Illinois policy that denied federally subsidized foster care payments to relatives and allowed them to qualify only for AFDC benefits. Case dismissed. • **1976:** Appeal to U.S. Supreme Court. Court directed federal court to reconsider case in light of DHHS administrative interpretation that states must provide federal foster care benefits to children placed in foster care with a relative. • **1976:** Federal District Court held that the Illinois policy violated federal law. • **1977:** Federal court of appeals ruled that federal district court was correct in holding that the Illinois policy violated federal law. • **1979:** U.S. Supreme Court ruled that federal Court of Appeals and federal District Court were correct in holding that Illinois policy violated federal law.	**1.** States cannot discriminate against kinship care parents in their payment policies under the federal Title IV-E foster care program. The federal foster care program covers children whom a court has determined have been abused or neglected and who have been placed with relatives who meet state licensing or approval requirements for foster homes. **2.** Under the court's holding, kinship parents must be paid the same as nonrelated foster parents when: • the child is eligible for AFDC and therefore eligible for Title IV-E; • the child's placement in foster care resulted from a judicial determination of abuse or neglect; • the child is under the responsibility of the state; and • the kinship home meets state licensing or approval requirements. **3.** The holding only applies if federal funding for foster care is involved.
Lipscomb v. Simmons 962 F.2d 1374 (9th Cir. 1992)	• **1989:** Case filed in federal District Court, challenging Oregon policy that denied state-financed foster care payments to children with relatives but provided them to children with nonrelative foster parents. Court upheld state's policy. • **1989:** Appeal to Ninth Circuit Court of Appeals. Court overruled federal District Court and held that denial of state-financed foster care payments to relatives violated children's constitutional rights. • **1990:** Ninth Circuit Court of Appeals agreed to rehear case.	**1.** Oregon policy that denies state-financed foster care payments to children with relatives but provides them to children with nonrelative foster parents does not violate children's constitutional rights. **2.** For equal protection purposes, heightened scrutiny by a court is required when legislative classifications disadvantage certain classes of individuals, such as classifications by race or national origin (called "suspect classes"). **3.** The court held that children in foster care do not constitute a

Case	Procedural History	Outcome / Notes
	• 1992: Ninth Circuit Court of Appeals affirmed the federal district court's original ruling that Oregon's policy was permissible.	"suspect class" and the Oregon policy was not entitled to heightened judicial scrutiny. All that was required was that Oregon have a "legitimate purpose" in denying foster care payments to relatives. Oregon stated, and the court agreed, that the "legitimate purpose" in denying the payments to relatives was that limited funds could be used for foster care for children who did not have relatives available to care for them.
King v. McMahon 230 Cal. Rptr. 911 (1986)	• 1986: Case filed in California state court, challenging California's policy of excluding children in kinship care from state financed foster care payments. Court held that policy was improper and children could not be excluded from foster care payments. • 1986: State Court of Appeals overturned the lower court's decision.	California has a legitimate purpose in denying state foster care benefits to children cared for by kin: "to achieve the goal of providing the maximum amount of needed foster care with available public funds."
Eugene F. v. Gross No. 1125/86 (N.Y. Sup Ct., filed 1986)	• 1986: Case filed in New York state court, seeking to force New York City to comply with state regulations establishing procedures and criteria for including relatives in the foster care system.	As of 1993, no final court decision. The case has, however, provided impetus for New York City's development of policies and practices regarding kinship care, including financial support, medical care, and other services, and the right to a fair hearing to request such support and services.
L.J. v. Massinga 838 F. 2d 118 (4th Cir. 1988)	• 1984: Case filed in federal District Court, alleging widespread systemic abuses in the Baltimore foster care system. Court issued a preliminary injunction against the Baltimore Department of Social Services, ordering changes in the system. • 1988: Fourth Circuit Court of Appeals upheld the District Court's order and agreed with the district court that the Department was not entitled to immunity from damages for harm suffered by children in foster care. • 1988: Baltimore Department of Social Services appealed to the U.S. Supreme Court. Court refused to hear the case. • 1988: Consent decree focusing on a range of issues, including kinship care, approved by the federal District Court.	Baltimore City Department of Social Services is required to reform its system to reduce caseload size, provide training to foster parents and caseworkers, monitor children's health care, ensure reporting of suspected abuse or neglect of children in care to the child's counsel, and improve the quality of services provided to kin who care for children in the child welfare system.

❧4❧
CRITICAL POLICY AND PRACTICE QUESTIONS

Existing kinship care policy and practice do not fully address a number of critical issues. Child welfare policy and program developers as well as practitioners continue to struggle with solutions to a range of concerns that impact kinship care policy and practice.

Balancing the Goals of Child Protection and Family Preservation

Because kinship care allows children to be cared for within their own families, it plays an important role as a family preservation service. Research suggests that kinship care families have many strengths that benefit children and their birth parents. The Task Force on Permanency Planning, for example, studied 100 kinship case records (representing 300 children) and found that the "majority of kinship care families...were poor but stable and hardworking families who cared about each other and could not understand the path that their children or siblings had chosen" [Task Force on Permanency Planning 1990: 9].

In a study by Thorton, social workers were asked how well children were faring in kinship care. A slight majority stated that, although kinship care could be problematic—especially in terms of the family/agency relationship—it was "good for the children." These benefits included not having the "stigma" of being a "foster child" and being able to maintain family ties and develop the positive identity that comes from belonging to a family of one's own [Thorton 1987: 63].

At the same time, however, kinship care raises concerns about the safety and well-being of the children for whom kin are caring, particularly in light of the intergenerational nature of child abuse and neglect, the intergenerational issues sometimes associated with substance abuse, and the continued access that parents may have to children who are living with kin. Other child protection issues relate to ongoing monitoring and supervision of kinship caregiving and the extent to which the safety of children can be assured without unnecessary intrusion into the lives of their families.

The ability of kin to ensure the safety of children and the extent to which state policies adequately address safety concerns present several major issues:

- When policies (such as relative preferences and waivers of licensing standards) facilitate placement of children with kin, does the assessment process adequately address child protection and safety needs?

- When policies permit less frequent casework visits to kin, is provision made for sufficient protection for the children, particularly in light of research findings that kinship homes are less likely to be approved or licensed and likely to be more accessible to parents than nonrelative foster homes?

- Are caseworkers adequately trained in the child protection and family preservation issues that kinship care, in contrast to nonrelative foster care, present?

- Are kinship caregivers adequately prepared and supported to enable them to ensure the safety of the

children while maintaining their relationships with
the children's birth parents?

Assuring Permanency for Children

Research has suggested that children cared for by kin tend to remain in
care longer than children in nonrelative foster care and that kin do not
usually adopt children placed with them [Benedict and White 1991;
Berrick et al. 1991; Wulczyn and Goerge 1991]. As the Task Force on
Permanency Planning noted, "while the most important issue is whether
the child feels secure in the caretaker setting, the intervention of the state
into family affairs calls for legal definitions and creates situations that are
difficult to address," including permanency. The Task Force found that
the permanency goal for most children in kinship care was "return to
parent" and that this goal was being stated year after year. In many cases,
there was no evidence of parental rehabilitation, the whereabouts of the
parents was unknown, or the mother was serving a long-term prison
sentence [Task Force on Permanency Planning 1990].

Title IV-E contains provisions that mandate permanency planning
for children in out-of-home care, but questions have arisen about the
extent to which permanency planning is actually being carried out with
children in kinship care and the appropriateness of these provisions for
children in kinship care. What "reasonable efforts" are required to reunite
children in kinship care with parents? Are the alternative permanency
planning options, particularly adoption, appropriate? When the placement with kin is stable, safe, and likely to last until the child reaches
adulthood, what is the appropriate ongoing role of the state in the lives
of the child and the family?

Financial Supports

Current policy and practice treats kinship parents in a variety of ways. The
financial support available to children cared for by kin depends on such
factors as:

- the state where the child and kin live;

- the child's eligibility for benefits under Title IV-E and AFDC;

- whether a state approves or licenses kinship homes; and

- whether kinship parents can meet state approval or licensing standards or other criteria applied to kinship care.

The financial benefits available to children cared for by kin may include foster care payments subsidized by the federal government, foster care payments wholly funded by state or local governments, AFDC benefits, child support payments; alternatively, there may be no public support whatsoever.

Issues of equity arise in a system where children in the custody of the public child welfare agency and cared for by kin are supported at a level different from that of those who are cared for by unrelated foster parents and where even among children in kinship care, the level of benefits differs. Several major questions arise:

1. What is an equitable and adequate level of financial support for children in kinship care? Some have argued that families have an obligation to "care for their own" and that a lower level of financial benefits for children in kinship care is indicated. Children in the custody of a public child welfare agency, however, whether cared for by kin or unrelated foster parents, require the same level of support and services to meet their basic and specialized needs. Additionally, research suggests that kin tend to have lower incomes and fewer resources than unrelated foster parents [Thorton 1987] and, as a result, children placed in such settings have a significant need for greater financial support.

2. What are the implications for children's return to birth parents when financial support is provided to kin at the foster care reimbursement rate? Because parents are not eligible to receive financial support for their children at the higher foster care reimbursement rate but rather at the lower AFDC rate, would a policy that reimburses kin at the foster care rate create incentives for parents to place their children with relatives in order to enhance the financial support available to them? Does a structure of lower AFDC payments for parents and higher foster care payments for kin create barriers to parent/child reunification?

3. *What are the implications for public funding when financial support is provided to children in kinship care at the same level as foster care?* Since kin are assuming a responsibility that would otherwise fall to the state if the children were placed in family foster care, what legitimate rationale is there for providing financial support for children in nonrelative foster care but denying such benefits to children in formal kinship care?

❦ Section III ❧
A FRAMEWORK
FOR THE FUTURE

"We are not asking for sympathy, everyone we know gives us that!...We are not asking for personal acknowledgment, because we are more than willing to help those whom we love. We are simply asking that you do what you can to make the laws more clear and more fair. If you do that, then we can help ourselves!"

—Letter from a grandparent to the
U.S. Senate Special Committee on Aging
Hearing on Grandparents Raising Grandchildren

❦ 5 ❦

GUIDING PRINCIPLES FOR POLICY
AND PRACTICE

The framework for kinship care policy and practice presented in this report is based on a recognition that kinship care is an essential child welfare service. The framework supports kinship care as the first option in the array of child welfare services that should be considered and assessed when a child is placed in the custody of a child welfare agency, either through court order or voluntarily by parents. The framework is based on a set of guiding principles.

1.   Every child's family, however family is defined (including nuclear, blended, extended, tribe or clan, or adoptive), is unique and has value, worth, integrity, and dignity.

2.   All families have strengths. Positive change is promoted when family strengths are supported while family needs are addressed.

3.   The most desirable place for children to grow up is in their own caring families, when those families are able to provide safe and nurturing relationships intended to last a lifetime.

4.   When children are placed with kin, child welfare agencies should

provide services to support the children's safety, growth, and healthy development. Children in formal kinship care are entitled to the same financial support services and protections that all children in the legal custody of the state receive.

5.   When children are placed with kin, child welfare agencies should support both the birth parents and kinship parents in their respective roles as nurturers, protectors, and teachers of the children in their care.

6.   Child welfare agencies should work to ensure kinship families access to support, enrichment, and crisis intervention services that are comprehensive, coordinated, culturally responsive, and community based.

7.   Child welfare agency staff members should recognize the different needs of the many racial, ethnic, and religious groups served by the child welfare system and should be competent in working with a racially and culturally diverse population.

❀6❀
COMPONENTS OF THE POLICY
AND PRACTICE FRAMEWORK

The framework for kinship care contains policy, program development, and practice recommendations in seven areas: assessment and approval/licensing; services for children, birth parents and kin; financial support for children in kinship care; preparation and support of kinship parents; monitoring and supervision; permanency planning; and other administrative issues.

Assessment and Approval/Licensing

An assessment of the willingness and ability of the prospective kinship parent to provide a safe, stable, nurturing home for a child for whom a child welfare agency has assumed responsibility is essential in order to ensure that the home can appropriately meet the child's needs. Approval/licensing of the kinship parent is critical. While this process must meet federal requirements in order for states to secure federal reimbursement for a portion of the costs associated with kinship care, states have flexibility to set separate standards for approval of kinship homes or to waive some designated requirements that apply to foster homes.

Available research, though limited, supports the willingness of kin to care for related children. A study of 1,000 African American children who entered out-of-home care in five cities in 1986 found that child welfare agencies frequently identify kin as a resource when children must be placed away from their parents, particularly in cases involving parental substance abuse [National Black Child Development Institute 1991]. The study found that in more than half of the cases, relatives offered to become the child's caregiver; among those who did not, the most often cited reasons were lack of financial ability, age, and existing obligations to care for other children. Some relatives were not approved by the child welfare agencies because of substance abuse by the relatives or concerns about future child abuse or neglect [National Black Child Development Institute 1991]. The Berkeley study obtained similar results. Almost 50 percent of the kin became caregivers at the agency's request; almost one-third had reported the abuse and neglect and volunteered to care for the child; and in the remaining cases, the child was already living with the relative when the formal placement was made [Berrick et al. 1991].

Assessment of the Kinship Family

An assessment of the willingness and ability of kin to provide a safe, stable, nurturing home and meet the child's developmental and safety needs is essential in determining the appropriateness of the home for the child for whom the agency has assumed legal responsibility. Assessment should be based on an understanding of the kinship family's culture and community, child-rearing approaches, and family dynamics, and should focus on the ability of the family to meet the immediate and ongoing needs of the child.

An assessment of the kinship family should include consideration of:

- The nature and quality of the relationship between the child and the relative;

- The ability and desire of the kinship parent to protect the child from further abuse or other maltreatment;

- The safety of the kinship home and the ability of kin to provide a nurturing environment for the child;

- The willingness of the kinship family to accept the child into the home;

- The ability of the kinship parent to meet the developmental needs of the child;

- The nature and quality of the relationship between the birth parent and the relative, including the birth parent's preference about placement of the child with kin;

- Any family dynamics in the kinship home related to the abuse or neglect of the child;

- The presence of alcohol or other drug involvement in the kinship home;

- The kinship family's willingness and ability to cooperate with the agency;

- The existing supports to which the kinship family has access;

- The number of children already being cared for by kin and the status of other children in the home, including their HIV status, their exposure to alcohol and other drugs, and their medical condition;

- The health status of the kinship parent(s);

- The age of the kinship parent(s) in light of the child's developmental and long-term needs; and

- When relevant, the possibility that family members will pressure the child to recant regarding disclosure of abuse.

As part of the assessment process, kinship parents should be assisted in understanding their role in working as partners with the child welfare agency and, when appropriate, the child's parents. Their role should be defined as:

- Protecting, nurturing, and caring for their kin children for a temporary or extended period of time;

- Assuring that the range of needs of the children who are placed with them are met;

- Helping return children to their parents whenever feasible; and

- When children cannot return to their parents, helping to establish a plan to connect children to safe, stable, nurturing family relationships intended to last a lifetime.

Recommendation

Child welfare agencies should use comprehensive, culturally competent assessment instruments to determine the ability of the kinship family to meet the needs of the child and to determine the family's strengths and needs in relation to assuming responsibility for the care of the child.

Actions

1. Train all kinship service staff to make comprehensive assessments of kinship families. Training should include in-depth preparation of new staff and enrichment training for experienced staff, updated and offered periodically.

2. Assess potential kinship families not as isolated entities, but in relation to the child, the child's parents, and the family.

3. Use a two-level assessment process: (1) a preplacement assessment focused on safety, protection, and the immediate health, educational, developmental, and emotional needs of the child in care and the willingness and ability of the kinship family to meet those needs; and

(2) a more in-depth assessment (within 45 days of the kinship care placement) focusing on the kinship parents' ability to meet the ongoing needs of the child and to engage in long-range planning for the child, identifying the concrete service needs of both the child and the kinship family, exploring permanency planning options for the child, and clearly defining the role and responsibilities of the kinship family and the social worker in supporting and strengthening the kinship care arrangement.

4. Assist kinship parents in assessing their abilities and preferences regarding the number of children for whom they can appropriately care.

5. Continue ongoing assessment throughout the service delivery process and not just in the "assessment phase."

Approval / Licensing of Kinship Homes

Approval/licensing ensures a basic level of quality care for children in the custody of the state. At the same time, approval/licensing is necessary to meet the requirements under Title IV-E for federal reimbursement for foster care maintenance payments for children who are Title IV-E eligible. Because approval/licensing plays a vital protective and financing role, it is essential that appropriate approval/licensing procedures be developed for kinship care.

The same standards regarding child protection and safety required for unrelated foster parents should apply in the approval and licensing of kinship parents. There should be flexibility, however, in applying standards unrelated to child protection and safety. With regard to these latter standards, agencies should consider separate criteria for approval of kinship homes or waiver of certain requirements that apply to unrelated foster families.

Recommendation

Child welfare agencies should require approval/licensing of kinship parents. Child welfare agencies should allow flexibility in determining the appropriateness of the kinship home, focusing on the protection of the child, the ability of the kinship parent(s) to provide for the child's needs, and the overall livability of the home.

Actions

1. Design family assessments and home studies for kinship parents that ensure the protection and safety of the child in kinship care and, at the same time, recognize the strengths of the kinship parents.

2. Utilize standards for evaluation of the physical safety of the kinship family home based on the housing quality standards set forth in the Section 8 program administered by the U.S. Department of Housing and Urban Development.

3. Require a complete check for criminal records and child protective service records for kinship parents and all adult members of the kinship household.

4. Disqualify potential kinship parents for offenses involving substantiated child abuse or neglect, sexual abuse, assault, and violent offenses involving minors. For other offenses, consider a process for a waiver of automatic disqualification under which a disqualifying offense could be weighed in relation to the age of the person at the time the offense was committed, the individual's history since the incident, the nature and seriousness of the offense in relation to possible risk to the child, whether the offense was a single incident or part of a pattern of conduct, and the social worker's assessment.

5. Build in flexibility regarding requirements related to the number of bedrooms, size and structure of the home, and amount of furniture, taking into account the developmental needs of the child for privacy and space. In relation to those requirements, offer services and supports, as appropriate, to assist the kinship family in adapting the home to meet the child's needs.

6. Build in flexibility regarding requirements related to the age and health of the kinship parent, taking into account the age and special needs of the child.

7. Clearly state to the potential kinship parent the child welfare agency

policy prohibiting the use of corporal punishment. This information should be presented early in the evaluation process. Attitudinal differences with this policy should be thoroughly examined in light of the kinship parent's age, educational background, cultural identity, and life experience. The agency should not approve/license the kinship home unless the kinship parent agrees to abide by the policy.

Services for Children, Birth Parents, and Kin

Despite the fact that children in kinship care and their kinship parents have equal, if not greater, service needs than their counterparts in family foster care, they are less likely to receive the services they need. The Berkeley study, for example, found that while 48 percent of children in traditional foster care were receiving mental health services at the time of the study, only 29 percent of children in kinship care were receiving such assistance [Berrick et al. 1991]. Likewise, researchers in the Baltimore study found that despite a high level of mental health needs, few children in kinship care had been evaluated for mental health problems and an even smaller number actually had received mental health services. The Baltimore researchers also noted that most children in kinship care had not received preventive health care, particularly dental, vision, and hearing screenings and care [Dubowitz 1990].

The research also suggests that needed specialized services are not readily available to children in kinship care. The Task Force on Permanency Planning discovered that children in kinship care often needed medical care and counseling services, but researchers could find little documentation in case records that indicated that the services were being received. Half the population studied involved drug-exposed infants, but there was no evidence in the case records that the infants were receiving the medical attention necessary to address their health and developmental needs [Task Force on Permanency Planning 1990].

Kinship parents are also unlikely to receive the services they need. The Berkeley study found that unrelated foster parents were more likely than kinship parents (23 percent versus 6 percent) to have access to respite care [Berrick et al. 1991]. The Burton study of grandparents in two urban areas found that a range of services was needed but not always available to kin: legal assistance, parenting programs, health care, counseling, support groups, and assistance in understanding and dealing with alcohol and other drug involved adult children [Burton 1992]. The Task Force on Permanency Planning also found that child care, parenting support, and counseling were among the services most often needed but often not available to kinship families [Task Force on Permanency Planning 1990].

Birth parents whose children are cared for by kin also lack needed services. As is the case with parents of children placed with unrelated foster parents, birth parents often need assistance in accessing a range of services, enhancing their parenting skills, and achieving the goals set forth in the case plan. These parents may find, for example, that alcohol and other drug treatments are unavailable, or they may be turned away because of a lack of resources or placed on a lengthy waiting list. Housing, income assistance, employment, job training, and counseling often are critical to reunification.

Just as services have been developed for children in their own homes and their parents, and for children in family foster care and their caregivers, services must be developed to address the range of needs of children in kinship care, their birth parents, and their kinship parents. These services, to a great extent, parallel the services needed by birth parents and foster parents and the children for whom they are caring, but certain aspects of the needed services must be adapted for kinship families. The following principles undergird the framework for kinship services:

- Children's developmental needs are paramount and must be met through a stable and nurturing environment and a range of services that address their physical, emotional, social, intellectual/educational and cultural needs;

- Family continuity is of value in promoting children's self-esteem, sense of heritage, and cultural connectedness;

- Cultural competence in kinship service design and delivery is essential. The design and delivery of kinship services must begin with an understanding of the need to respond respectfully and effectively to people of all cultures, classes, races, ethnic backgrounds, and religions in a manner that recognizes, affirms, and values the worth of individuals, families, and communities and protects and preserves the dignity of each person [CWLA 1992]. Kinship care services must be developed with an understanding and appreciation of the culture of the children and families that the agency serves.

- Kinship programs should have a philosophy of family empowerment, emphasize family strengths in a nondeficit manner, utilize a capacity-building approach, and offer a range of services from preventive to rehabilitative designed to support and strengthen children, birth parents, and kinship parents.

Kinship services may be provided by staff specifically assigned to kinship care programs. Separate kinship programs, however, may not always be feasible. In such cases, efforts should be made to ensure that children in kinship care, their birth parents, and their kin receive the attention they need.

Services for Children in Kinship Care

Kinship care services must meet the range of needs of children cared for by kin. All children have the need for protection and nurturing that promotes growth and development. Positive family relationships, including those through kinship ties, promote children's feelings of being loved, wanted, worthwhile, capable, and responsible, and should be supported and enhanced. At the same time, children in kinship care have a range of needs related to their physical and emotional health, personal, and social development, and education which must be addressed with appropriate and responsive services.

Recommendation

Child welfare agencies should develop a comprehensive array of services designed to meet the protective, health, emotional, educational, social, religious, and relationship needs of children and should work collaboratively with kinship parents to ensure that children receive all needed services.

Actions

1. Ensure that staff recognize and respond to the special child protection issues in kinship care and provide ongoing assessment and monitoring of kinship care placements.

2. Obtain the commitment of kinship parents to insuring the safety of the child in kinship care.

3. Ensure that staff follow reporting requirements, policies, and procedures when there is suspected risk of child maltreatment in kinship care.

4. Assess the physical, developmental, emotional and social needs of each child in kinship care in consultation with the birth parent and the kinship parent and develop a service plan to ensure that those needs are met. Monitor progress in meeting the child's needs.

5. Assist kinship parents in meeting children's needs concerning separation, loss, and grief.

6. Involve children to the extent possible in case planning and implementation.

7. Advocate for the child as well as the birth parents and kinship parents in negotiating with other service systems and brokering access to resources for the child and family members.

Services for Parents

The service needs of parents vary in nature, scope, and intensity. All parents need assistance in understanding the precipitating factors that made kinship care necessary, working cooperatively with the kinship service worker and the kinship parent in determining the service goals and the plan for achieving those goals, and carrying out the agreed-upon tasks and responsibilities as well as any requirements established by the court. Parents may also need assistance in obtaining resources such as housing, substance abuse treatment, job skills training, employment, parenting education, health services, and budgeting. Parents should be assisted in participating in their children's lives in a positive and appropriate manner that is consistent with the permanency plan for the child. Parents also may need help in identifying and resolving areas of conflict with kinship parents.

Recommendation
Child welfare agencies should provide the services that parents need for support, rehabilitation, and enhancement of their functioning as parents.

Actions

1. Assist parents in addressing the problems that led to their child's placement in kinship care and the services they need to remedy those problems.

2. Provide appropriate services to parents to achieve reunification whenever possible.

3. Include within the case plan for each child in kinship care a structured schedule of visits to help in the reunification process and at the same time assess whether reunification will be possible.

4. Proactively reach out to parents, consistently giving the message that they are important to the child and that they have a responsibility to the child.

5. Involve parents in case planning and implementation.

6. Make a concerted effort to include fathers in the assessment and plan for ongoing services and incorporate their input into the formal service agreement.

7. Invite parents to participate in family meetings to assess progress in implementing the plan for the child and family toward achievement of the permanency planning goals.

8. When reunification of the child with the parent is not feasible, provide counseling to the parents regarding voluntary relinquishment and termination of parental rights.

Services for Kinship Families

When kin take on the parenting role, it is usually unplanned. Kin come forward to care for children because of the strength of family ties, a sense of obligation to care for their own, a refusal to allow children to live with people they do not know, or an assurance they gave to the parents. Caring for children, however, may place emotional and financial stress on kin as they take on full-time parenting roles. At the same time, the relationship between kin and the child's parents may be complex. Kin may feel responsible for helping the child's parents with personal problems and troubles, emotionally burdened with the responsibility of "holding it all together" for both the parents and the child, guilty because of the child's abuse or neglect by other family members, doubtful about the quality of their own parenting, or frustrated with their adult children and unwilling to continue any involvement between the child and the child's parents.

Recommendation

Child welfare agencies should provide kin with the supports and services they need to meet the child's needs, assist the child's parents, and meet their own needs as caregivers.

Actions

1. View the kinship care parents not only as "providers" of services but as members of the family. Avoid references to the kinship family as a *placement.*

2. Include the kinship parents as a part of the team of service providers and involve them in case planning and implementation.

3. Assist the kinship parents in providing the child with nurturing care and in meeting the child's ongoing physical, developmental, and emotional needs.

4. Assess and respond to the emotional support and concrete service needs of the kinship family in planning and maintaining the kinship care arrangement.

5. Assist the kinship family in obtaining the services they need, including access to health care coverage for the children in their care, day care, respite care, homemaker services, transportation, counseling, guidance, and help with stress management.

6. Assist the kinship parents in addressing the impact of the abuse and/ or neglect of the children in their care.

7. Assist the kinship parents in addressing alcohol and other drug (AOD) issues that affect the children in their care and issues related to the birth parents' AOD abuse/dependency if appropriate.

8. Communicate clearly to the kinship parents the requirements related to agency monitoring and supervision.

9. Work collaboratively with the kinship parents to prevent/avert crises by mobilizing needed intensive services such as mental health evaluations and treatment, health care, and hospitalization.

10. Support kinship families in identifying and using self-help resources.

11. Send agency representatives to community meetings to learn about the effectiveness of existing kinship care service programs and help kinship parents maximize the benefits of such programs.

12. Form liaisons with public and private community agencies that provide preventive and supportive services to families and expedite referrals for kinship families when needed.

13. Establish a kinship care service advisory committee with community and kinship parent members.

Financial Support for Children in Kinship Care

Children in the legal custody of public child welfare agencies have a range of needs for which financial support is essential. Research on the financial support of children placed with kin indicates that a primary service need of kinship families is additional financial support [Dubowitz 1990; Burton 1992]. At present, state policies governing the payment of foster care maintenance for children in kinship care vary widely. Most states provide financial support for children placed with kin only if the kinship parents are officially approved or licensed. In some states, federal funds and matching state funds are used to support the care of Title IV-E eligible children by kin under the foster care program. In other states, however, there are prohibitions on using state and local funds to support children in kinship care. In those instances, the only available form of public support is Aid to Families with Dependent Children (AFDC). If the child is not AFDC eligible, no public support may be available, and kinship families must use their own financial resources to meet the needs of children placed with them.

The legal and policy framework for kinship care is based on the principle that financial support—whether federally, state, or locally-based—must follow the child who is placed under the legal responsibility of the child welfare agency, whether the child is placed with nonrelated foster parents or with kin.

In addition, adequate financial support for children in kinship care must extend beyond providing financial benefits to support the ongoing care of children. Child welfare agencies also should ensure that children in their legal custody access the benefits for which they are eligible under other federally-supported programs, including Medicaid, Supplemental Security Income (SSI), and child support through Title IV-D of the Social Security Act.

Recommendation

Each state should determine the level of support to be provided for children in the legal custody of the public child welfare agency, and provide that level of support for all children in out-of-home care, including children in kinship care. Financial support should be set at a level appropriate to meet children's physical, mental health, and developmental needs.

Actions

1. Implement policies and procedures that establish a uniform level of child welfare benefits for all children in the legal custody of the public child welfare agency.

2. Develop a clear statement of the financial support that is available to children in kinship care.

3. Clearly define the rights and responsibilities of kinship parents upon approval or licensing of their homes, including access to financial support for the children for whom they are caring.

    ### Recommendation
    Child welfare agencies should ensure that children in kinship care have access to the range of benefits available under federal programs for which they are eligible.

    ### Action

1. Develop and implement procedures to ensure that children in kinship care receive Medicaid, Supplemental Security Income (SSI), child support payments, and other benefits available under federal programs to which they are entitled.

2. Provide assistance and support to kinship parents in applying for benefits for their kin children.

Preparation and Support of Kinship Parents

The limited research that has looked at the training of kinship parents indicate that few relatives are formally prepared for their role and responsibilities as caregivers. In the Berkeley study, researchers learned that 76 percent of nonrelative foster parents received general training, compared to only 13 percent of kinship caregivers. Fifty-nine percent of nonrelative foster parents received specialized training, including training regarding caring for drug-involved children, but only five percent of kin received such training. The study also found that foster parents were more likely to have access to support groups than kinship parents (62 percent versus 15 percent) [CRS 1993].

Kinship parents must be prepared to assure the safety and well-being of the child, to meet the child's specialized needs, and to manage their relationship and contact with the child's parent. Orientation programs can be used to help kinship parents obtain the competencies necessary to meet the needs of children in kinship care and to work collaboratively with the agency in case planning and implementation. Discussion groups can be used to provide a forum for kinship parent education and an opportunity for kinship parents to address common situations they encounter. Framing this preparation and support in terms of orientation programs and discussion groups avoids the use of the term *training,* which some kinship parents may perceive as disrespectful given the fact that in many instances, they have raised at least one generation of children.

In addition to orientation programs and discussion groups, support groups can play an important ongoing role for kinship parents. These groups may be organized and run by kinship parents, facilitated by child welfare staff, or both.

Recommendation

Child welfare agencies should develop orientation programs and discussion groups to ensure that kinship parents are prepared to meet the needs of the children for whom they are caring, to manage their relationships with the children's parents, and to work effectively with the agency.

Actions

1. Ensure that orientation programs and discussion programs are available to kinship parents.

2. Ensure that orientation programs and discussion groups address the following issues, among others:

    - the developmental needs of children;

    - the impact of abuse and neglect on the children in kinship care;

    - the dynamics of loss and grieving as they relate to the child, the birth parents, and the kinship parent;

    - the shift in patterns of authority and responsibility between the birth parent and the kinship parent as a result of the kinship care arrangement;

    - the role of the kinship parent as a change agent

within the family to address issues that precipitated placement;

- building the child's self-esteem;

- the role of the kinship parent as a model for positive parenting;

- alcohol and other drug (AOD) issues, including the prenatal and environmental impact of parental AOD abuse on children, the management of challenges posed by chemically involved children, the issues involved in birth parents' AOD abuse/dependency, and management of the relationship and contact with the chemically dependent parent;

- adolescent pregnancy and teenage sexuality issues;

- HIV/AIDS;

- meeting children's special medical and educational needs;

- the relationships among kinship siblings and other children in the household;

- issues specific to kinship parenting, including the stresses of full-time parenting for the second time, and the dynamics involved in parenting young children as an older adult;

- agency requirements and expectations relating to monitoring and supervision and permanency planning; and

- agency policies and procedures that affect kinship parents.

3. Encourage and offer assistance to kinship parents to lead or co-lead discussion groups.

Recommendation

Child welfare agencies should develop or work with community-based organizations to develop support groups for kinship parents.

Actions

1. Ensure that support groups are available for kinship parents and that kinship parents are encouraged to participate.

2. Assist kinship parents in connecting with local, state, or national kinship parent organizations that focus on support and/or advocacy for kinship parents.

3. Refer parents to the Association of Retired Persons (AARP) Grandparent Information Center, which collects and disseminates pertinent information for all kinship parents, not only grandparents.

Recommendation

Child welfare agencies should develop opportunities for kinship parents to convey their needs and concerns to agency administrators.

Actions

1. Hold periodic meetings with kinship parents to identify their areas of concern.

2. Include within orientation programs and discussion groups opportunities for kinship parents to talk with agency administrators.

Monitoring and Supervision

The Inspector General's report indicates that most states' policies require less supervision and monitoring of kinship parents than unrelated foster families, even though children in kinship care are more likely to be in unlicensed homes [HHS Inspector General 1992]. Research likewise indicates that kinship parents and the children for whom they are caring have less contact with social workers than unrelated foster parents and the children placed with them. The Berkeley study found that 27 percent of kinship parents reported no contact with a social worker in a one month period as compared with 19 percent of unrelated foster parents. More than one-third of the kin stated that they wanted more contact with social workers and 45 percent believed better communication with the agency would be helpful [Berrick et al. 1991]. Research also suggests that birth parents whose children are in kinship care tend to have more contact with their children than those whose children are in family foster care. The Berkeley research, for example, found that contact with birth parents occurred in 81 percent of the kinship care families as compared with 58 percent of the unrelated foster families. Parent visits in kinship care were more likely to be directly arranged between parents and kin while the agency most often arranged visits when children were in family foster care [Berrick et al. 1991]. The ongoing contact between birth parents and their children in kinship care is important from a permanency planning and family preservation perspective, but the absence of monitoring and supervision raises protection and safety issues.

Research suggests that monitoring and supervision of kinship homes has presented special challenges for child welfare agencies. Social workers in Thorton's study [1987], for example, reported that kinship caregivers were more difficult to supervise than foster parents. They noted that kinship caregivers tended to be uncomfortable with agency supervision, did not always comply with agency policies, and experienced authority conflicts with the agency. Thorton also found, however, that workers' views were significantly influenced by (1) their position in the agency, (2) their length of employment at the agency, and (3) the size of their caseload. Those workers who had direct contact with kinship parents and were not supervisors and/or administrators tended to view kinship parents as less problematic [Thorton 1987].

The Task Force on Permanency Planning [1990] found little evidence in the case records studied that agencies were complying with regulatory requirements regarding caseworker supervision of kinship care homes. The Task Force suggested three possible explanations for this: (1) caseworkers were assuming that kinship homes did not require as much supervision as nonrelative foster care homes because the child was placed with relatives; (2) relatives were viewing caseworkers' home studies and supervision as intrusive; and (3) the child welfare system, already in crisis, was not able to respond to the rapid increase in caseload sizes, and as a result, was unable to provide the ongoing monitoring and supervision that was needed [Task Force on Permanency Planning 1990].

Monitoring and supervision of the placement of children in the custody of the state are critical social work activities. They are essential to the protection of children in kinship care and to the ongoing support of the kin who are caring for them.

Recommendation

Child welfare agencies should require regular and frequent contacts between the agency social worker and the child and kinship parent to continually address the health, safety, and well-being of the child and the service needs of the kinship family.

Actions

1. Limit caseload size to 12 to 15 children per caseworker to ensure that an appropriate level of monitoring and supervision is provided to the child, the birth parent, and the kinship parent.

2. Require social work visits in the kinship family home at least once a month, with additional personal and telephone contacts as needed to monitor the health, safety, and well-being of the child and to meet the service needs of the child and kinship caregiver.

3. Set procedures for written documentation of the child's health, safety, and well-being; contacts with the child and kinship parent; progress in achieving the goals outlined in the case plan; progress toward achieving the permanency plan for the child; and current case status.

Permanency Planning

Children in kinship care, like all children, need safe, nurturing relationships intended to last a lifetime. Permanency planning services are as essential for children in kinship care as for children in family foster care. To the extent possible, the permanent plan should be developed collaboratively by the birth parent, the kinship parent, the caseworker, and the child, when age appropriate.

Research suggests that permanency planning for children in kinship care differs significantly from permanency planning for children in family foster care. Several studies have indicated that children placed with kin remain in care for longer periods of time than children in family foster care [Benedict and White 1991; Berrick et al. 1991; Wulczyn and Goerge 1991]. In a study that compared children in 95 active kinship care cases in New York City in April 1985 with children in foster care, researchers found very different permanency goals [Thorton 1991]. Children in kinship care more often had a goal of "discharge to independent living," a status that generally meant long-term foster care, and very seldom had a goal of either return to their parents or adoption. When researchers asked 20 kinship families about adoption, they learned that kin generally were not willing to adopt, even with adoption subsidies, but were willing to care for children on a long-term basis until they grew up. Most kin felt that because they and the children already were a family, adoption was unnecessary. Several kin also expressed concern that adoption would harm their relationship with the children's parents [Thorton 1991].

Research also suggests that kin and social workers view the permanency plans for children quite differently. In the Baltimore study, social workers stated that more than one-third of the children would return to their parents but kin believed only one-fifth of the children would do so. Social workers indicated that in almost 60 percent of the cases, children would remain with kin. Kin, however, thought that the children would remain with them in less than 40 percent of the cases [Dubowitz 1990]. Differences also appear in the research comparing the expectations of kinship parents and foster parents. In the Berkeley study, researchers found that kin more often expect children to remain in care until they grow up, while foster parents are more likely to expect children to be adopted. Expectations regarding return home to parents also varied. Among caregivers who expected that their children would leave care, 52 percent of the kinship parents believed children would return to their parents, but only 28 percent of the foster parents held that belief [Berrick et al. 1991].

Research also indicates that visits between birth parents and children, one of the most important determinants in reunification, occur more frequently for children in kinship care than for children in family foster care. In one study, researchers found that 56 percent of the children in the kinship homes saw their birth parents at least once a month, as compared to 32 percent of children in family foster care during the same time period. Nearly one-fifth (19 percent) of children in kinship care saw their birth parents more than four times a month while very few (3 percent) of the children in family foster care did so [Berrick et al. 1991].

The observed differences between permanency planning for children in kinship care and family foster care have been attributed to a number of factors: the relationship between kinship parents and the birth parents; the nature and quality of the relationship between the kinship parents and the child welfare agency; and the child welfare system's response to kinship arrangements as less urgent and requiring less attention than family foster care.

No single legal procedure will be appropriate to formalize permanency in all kinship care cases. Several alternatives must be available: return to parents, adoption by kin, guardianship with kin, long-term kinship care and nonrelated adoption. When the plan is for kinship care to be temporary, criteria must be established for case review, agency supervision, and evaluation of efforts toward reunification with parents, and time-limited goals must be set. When the plan is for kinship care to be permanent, criteria should be established for the kinship parents to obtain legal custody. If kinship care is to be long-term with agency supervision, the situation may be similar to long-term foster care and the appropriate level of agency supervision, case review, and services must be planned. When neither reunification with parents nor permanent care by kin is feasible, adoption by nonrelatives must be considered.

Reunification with Parents

The first option in permanency planning is reunification with parents whenever feasible. As with all children in care, children in kinship care and kinship parents should be aware of the plan for reunification as soon after placement as possible, and should participate in a structured plan of visits between the child and the child's parents and siblings. Child welfare agencies must make reasonable efforts to reunite children and their birth parents, offering a range of services to assist parents in resolving the problems that led to the placement of the child in kinship care. Kinship parents are partners with the agency in facilitating reunification efforts. They can be effective mentors and role models for parents in demonstrating appropriate parenting behaviors and positive discipline techniques.

Recommendation

Child welfare agencies should consider reunification with parents as the preferred permanency planning goal for children in kinship care and make reasonable efforts to reunify children with their parents.

Actions

1. In the initial assessment and on an ongoing basis, explore and evaluate the feasibility of reunifying the child with the parents;

2. Begin permanency planning at the time of placement and, when appropriate, work toward reunification with parents.

3. Thoroughly discuss the permanency plan for the child with the kinship parent.

4. Include specific plans for contacts and visits with parents and siblings and the rules that will govern visits.

Permanency with Kin

When children cannot be reunited with their parents, efforts should be made whenever possible to keep children in kinship care with their kinship parents [Takas 1993]. Kinship care arrangements should be preserved when they are safe, nurturing, and stable. Permanency, whenever possible, should be assured through a legal status for the child such as adoption or guardianship or through long-term kinship care.

Recommendation

Child welfare agencies should recognize permanency with kin as a permanency option that carries with it services to preserve the kinship care relationship.

Actions

1. When reunification with parents is not feasible, determine whether the kinship parent is able to continue to provide a safe, stable, nurturing home for the child in kinship care.

2. Determine whether the kinship parent is willing to make a permanent commitment to the care of the child through adoption, guardianship, or long-term kinship care.

3. Determine and provide for the needs of the kinship family when the family is able and willing to provide a permanent home for the child, including legal services to help obtain custody or guardianship and financial support for the care of the child.

Permanency with kin through adoption. Adoption provides a stable legal status for the child with adults who assume parental rights and responsibilities. Adoption by kin provides legal protections for children; promotes continuity of relationships with the child's family and culture; and gives the kinship parent authority to secure health care, change educational programs, and make other major decisions regarding the child.

Adoption also facilitates access to a range of benefits for the child. Children of adoptive kinship parents are entitled to their adoptive kinship parent's social security benefits and to enrollment in their adoptive kinship parents' health insurance benefits. In addition, they are legally entitled to inherit from their adoptive kinship parents. Children adopted by kinship parents may be eligible for an adoption subsidy that provides financial assistance to meet the child's special needs after the adoption is finalized.

Adoption by kin, however, has been problematic as a permanency plan in kinship care. Adoption requires the termination of the rights of the birth parents, followed by the full assumption of parental rights and responsibilities by the adoptive family. As a result, some kin have been reluctant to pursue adoption, finding it undesirable in terms of its potential impact on their relationship with the child's birth parents. Alternatively, some kin believe adoption to be unnecessary in light of existing family relationships.

Reports from child welfare agencies, however, suggest that an increasing number of kinship parents may be interested in adopting children in their care. More kin appear to be viewing adoption as a way of securing their parenting role and ensuring that the parents or the child welfare agency will not have the authority to separate the child from them. Increasingly, parents' voluntary relinquishment of children for adoption by kin is being considered in planning for permanence, particularly by parents with HIV/AIDS or other health problems, or those who face an extended period of incarceration.

Adoption has become more relevant to kinship care as the concept of open adoption has gained acceptance. Increasingly, the termination of parents' custody rights does not necessarily terminate parents' relationships with their children. Agencies are now working with adoptive families, birth parents, and children to explore the appropriate extent of continued post-adoption involvement of birth parents with their children through visits or other forms of contact.

Recommendation

When return to parents is not feasible, child welfare agencies should assess the appropriateness of adoption by kin as the permanent plan for the child.

Actions

1. Develop policies that support adoption by kin as a permanent plan for the child when return to parents is not appropriate.

2. Provide parents with counseling and support regarding adoption as an option for their children, including information on voluntary relinquishment, open adoption, and adoption by designated kin.

3. Provide the kinship parent with counseling and support regarding adoption, including information on adoption subsidies.

4. Provide ongoing, periodic post-legal adoption services and supports to kin to maintain the child's well-being and family stability.

Permanency with kin through guardianship. Guardianship provides a means for kin to assume parental responsibility and authority without permanently severing parental rights. Guardianship gives kinship parents the authority to consent to health care for the child, change educational programs, and make certain decisions for the child. Guardianship requires court authorization and is subject to possible termination when parents seek to regain their full authority over the child.

Legal guardianship is often more acceptable to kinship parents than adoption because it does not involve terminating the rights of the child's parents. Generally, however, it carries with it no public financial support as would the adoption of a child with special needs. The absence of subsidies to support guardianship arrangements has been identified as a barrier to achievement of permanency for many children in kinship care. Many kinship families report that they choose to remain in the formal child welfare system because they need the financial support available through the foster care program to continue to care for children. These benefits would end if custody were transferred from the agency to kin through a guardianship arrangement.

Permanency with kin through kin guardianship would be enhanced as an option if subsidies were available. A barrier to the provision of a guardianship subsidy, however, has been that there are no federal provisions for federal matching funds for a permanency plan of guardianship. At present, the provision of a guardianship subsidy is only available through use of state or local funds. Illinois, for example, provides a form of subsidized guardianship, known as *successor guardianship*, for the kinship guardians of children who formerly were in foster care with relatives. New York, Maryland, and other states are considering similar provisions. The recent report of the Office of Inspector General of the U.S. Department of Health and Human Services, has recommended that the federal government consider expanding the existing federal special needs adoption subsidy program to include special needs guardianship. Critical steps in enhancing guardianship as a permanent plan for children in kinship care are federal recognition of guardianship as a permanency option for children in kinship care and federal matching funding of special needs guardianship.

Recommendation

Child welfare agencies should promote subsidized guardianship by kin as an acceptable permanency plan.

Actions

1. Advocate for a subsidized guardianship program to support permanency for children in kinship care.

2. Promote changes in federal law and regulations to allow for federal reimbursement for guardianship subsidies similar to the subsidized adoption assistance program.

3. Provide ongoing, periodic services and support to kin who opt for guardianship to maintain child well-being and family stability.

Long-Term Kinship Care

For a limited number of children, long-term kinship care is the most appropriate option in the same way that long-term foster care is most appropriate for some children. Long-term kinship care may be indicated when children are in need of continuing services in addition to the financial supports that are available only if they remain in the formal kinship care system. Long-term kinship care may also be appropriate when kinship parents are unable to make long-term financial commitments to the care of the child; when there is a need for the protections offered by the child welfare agency with regard to child safety, custody, and court protection; or when birth parents, kinship parents, the child, or the court are reluctant to approve other plans for permanence.

Recommendation

Child welfare agencies should make provisions for the use of long-term kinship care as an acceptable permanency plan for children when appropriate.

Actions

1. Include long-term kinship care in the array of acceptable permanency plans for children in kinship care.

2. Develop guidelines and parameters for establishing and documenting why a plan of long-term kinship care is most appropriate for a child.

3. Include in the planning process the financial and service benefits that children in long-term kinship care will need.

Non-Relative Adoption

When it is necessary for a child to be separated from his or her birth parents and kin, adoption by a nonrelative represents the best remaining alternative for the child. Adoption by a new, unrelated family offers a secure, nurturing environment necessary for optimal growth and development and one that protects the child's legal and inheritance rights. Adoptive relationships also have a greater potential for providing continuity and support throughout adulthood than do temporary arrangements such as extended foster care.

Adoption has become a more attractive alternative for children in kinship care as the concept of open adoption has gained greater acceptance. While open adoptions vary considerably in the form and frequency of contact between birth families and adoptive families, reports from children, birth parents, and adoptive parents about the benefits of open adoption are encouraging. Open adoption allows birth families to view voluntary relinquishment of their parental rights—or involuntary termination of those rights—as not necessarily terminating their relationship with their child. Open adoption allows them to keep abreast of their child's growth and development. Children in open adoptions may be able to deal with the reality of their adoption more easily, and adoptive parents may find greater satisfaction in their role as adoptive parents. Open adoption is not always possible, however, particularly in situations involving a pattern of violence, serious mental illness, or extensive substance abuse. In these cases, the problems within the birth family may be too severe and their ability to negotiate and maintain an open adoption agreement too limited. Nevertheless, large numbers of families, many of whom were foster parents initially, are currently experimenting with a range of open adoption alternatives. Similar arrangements may be possible between nonrelated adoptive families and kin. In the context of kinship care, child welfare agencies need to recruit and prepare a pool of families willing to participate in open adoption and support adoptive families as they deal with the special complexities that kin relationships may present following adoption.

Recommendation

When return to parents or permanency with kin is not feasible, child welfare agencies should secure a new, unrelated adoptive family for the child.

Actions

1. Develop policies that support nonrelative adoption as a permanent plan for a child when return to the parent or permanency with the kinship family is not appropriate.

2. Recruit a pool of culturally diverse potential adoptive families and prepare them for any special needs the children have.

3. Provide a range of post-placement and post-adoption supports, subsidies, and services for families who adopt to maintain the child's well-being and family stability.

Other Administrative Issues

Little if any research exists on the extent to which social workers are prepared to work with kinship families or assist in their ongoing work with kin. Though not directly indicative of staff training or preparation, the Berkeley study found that kin tend to have less contact with caseworkers than unrelated foster parents and have a more positive view of them [Berrick et al. 1991]. Like unrelated foster parents, kin stated that their relationships with social workers could be improved; foster parents, however, tended to be more dissatisfied with the type and frequency of contacts and communication with social workers [Berrick et al. 1991]. These studies suggest that caseworkers may already possess a range of skills that are viewed positively by kinship parents.

The quality of kinship care programs will rest on the preparation of social workers to assess and address the needs of children, birth parents, and kin in kinship care; the ongoing support provided to social workers as they address the specific issues that arise in the context of kinship care; and the nature and quality of the information that is made available to social workers as well as program developers so that kinship care programs can be monitored and improved. The ability of social workers to work effectively with kinship families is enhanced by competency-based training, staff supports, appropriate caseload size, and recognition of quality work. At the same time, information management is essential to understanding program outcomes and maximizing program responsiveness and effectiveness. Finally, coordination of services both within the agency and with other agencies that serve children, birth parents, and kin is critical to effective service delivery.

Competency-Based Training and Other Supports for Staff

Specialized training programs for kinship service staff and staff support are essential to quality kinship care programs. In order to work effectively with children and families in kinship care, social workers must be able to convey a strong commitment to the needs and best interests of the child in care as well as to the whole family, and must be able to develop a partnership with the parent and the kinship parent.

Successfully maintaining a focus on the best interests of the child within the context of the family in kinship care requires that the worker have a range of competencies including, but not limited to, the following abilities:

- Convey respect for the kinship family.

- Demonstrate an awareness and acceptance of human differences and the role that culture plays in motivating human behavior; an ability and willingness to build upon a cultural knowledge base; and an ability to engage in a culturally responsive practice.

- Fully understand and have strong clinical skills in relation to separation, attachment, and loss.

- Assess with the family their strengths and needs, and how each family member can participate in the problem-solving process.

- Set goals with the family that all family members understand and that are tailored to the strengths and needs of each individual family member.

- Monitor with the family progress toward goals and make changes as appropriate.

- Negotiate and resolve conflicts, assisting family members in creating the necessary structure to facilitate positive communication and interaction.

- Assist family members in working through parent-child and sibling issues that impede problem-solving.

- Provide or arrange for needed essential services, such as food, clothing, housing, utilities, and child day care.

- Assist the family in developing and using resources in their community and mobilizing the necessary supports to achieve their goals.

To provide effective kinship care services, staff must participate in competency-based pre-service and in-service training and strong supervisory leadership must be available. Supervisors need to learn and implement a style of supervision that models child-centered, family-focused work, a style characterized by greater staff participation, frequent staffing of cases, attention to systemic barriers that may be impairing the workers' ability to work with children and families, and advocacy to ensure that social workers are receiving the support and resources they need to achieve the best possible outcomes for children and their families.

Recommendation

Child welfare agencies should provide ongoing comprehensive competency-based training for social workers who are working in kinship care programs.

Actions

1. Involve social workers in identifying the needed competencies.

2. Support staff in acquiring the competencies they need through pre-service and in-service training, contracting for specialized training on such issues as alcohol or other drug dependency, circulation of current professional journals and articles, and opportunities to attend and participate in conferences.

Recommendation

Child welfare agencies should seek collaborative training with other key decision makers who develop and act upon child welfare policy, make child welfare decisions, and allocate resources, including judges and attorneys, court officers, medical and mental health professionals, law enforcement personnel, and educators.

Actions

1. Arrange for multidisciplinary participation in training to enhance all participants' understanding of the policy and practice issues involved in kinship care, the special needs of children in kinship care, and the importance of involving the whole family in problem-solving.

2. Involve key decision makers in periodic and ongoing dialogue about how best to provide support and services to children and their families in kinship care arrangements.

Recommendation

Child welfare agencies should establish a caseload size of 12 to 15 children per caseworker providing kinship care service.

Actions

1. Communicate an awareness that provision of quality kinship care

services to children, parents, and kinship parents requires a manageable caseload.

2. Establish a system of case assignment and transfer that promotes adherence to the caseload limits.

3. Communicate to advisory boards, governors, commissioners, mayors, state legislatures, and other appropriate governing bodies the necessity of maintaining the caseload limit.

Recommendation
Child welfare agencies should develop supports for staff to enhance their ability to provide quality services to children, birth parents, and kin.

Actions

1. Develop flexible discretionary or emergency funding that staff members may use for essential services or items to assist kin in meeting the child's immediate needs or for ongoing services such as day care or counseling.

2. Utilize consultants to assist social workers in evaluating and meeting specialized treatment needs, such as needs for psychological evaluation and treatment, alcohol and drug treatment, special education and health care.

3. Develop service teams to deliver a broad range of child welfare services.

Recommendation
Child welfare agencies should establish a process of recognition of excellence in the performance of kinship service provision.

Actions

1. Develop a process for regular recognition of staff who do outstanding work.

2. Reward staff who achieve and maintain a high level of competence. The selection process could include recommendations by adminis-

trative staff, peer elections, and/or nominations from the kinship families.

Information Management

To date, it has been difficult to obtain data regarding kinship care. Kinship care has not been defined precisely and it has been difficult to identify and count accurately the number of children living with kin. Because data is lacking, it has been impossible to evaluate program effectiveness and service needs. The development of kinship care programs should include developing and tracking relevant data to assist in the planning of kinship programs and evaluation of kinship care in terms of outcomes for children.

Recommendation

Child welfare agencies should plan for and implement procedures for computerized tracking and management of kinship care information.

Actions

1. Develop a data tracking system that includes but is not limited to the numbers of children in kinship care; the demographics of kinship families; length of time in kinship care; kinship services provided; kinship service needs; primary health care needs; Early and Periodic Screening, Diagnosis, and Treatment (EPSDT) visits; and the permanency goal for each child in kinship care.

2. Implement a management information system for tracking the status of individual children in kinship care.

Program Coordination

Kinship care programs will be effective when well-coordinated with other child welfare services, including family preservation services, child protective services, family foster care, group and residential care, and adoption, as well as with other service delivery systems, including income maintenance, housing, public health, mental health, and education.

Recommendation

*Child welfare agencies should coordinate services at both an intra-
and interagency level to ensure effective, timely service provision,
and a smooth transition when case transfer between programs is
required.*

Actions

1. Establish a system of case transfer with time requirements that assure
   continuity of services for kinship families with a minimum of
   disruption.

2. Enable caseworkers who transfer and who receive cases to have case
   conferences and provide joint visits for a time-limited period to avoid
   gaps in services and ensure an appropriate transition.

3. Explain to kinship families the differences between programs and
   services that will affect them, such as the move from child protection
   services to kinship care or foster care.

4. Establish an aftercare service program for kinship families who have
   moved into their permanent arrangement, but need temporary
   services to assist them in their passage to kinship care without
   supervision of the child welfare agency.

❧ Section IV ❧
NEXT STEPS

"[We must]...forge a new approach to children...and forge a bond between Washington and local government. It can't be Washington saying we know best. It's got to be us asking the people—communities—what the problems are and what the best solutions are."

—The Honorable Janet Reno
Attorney General of the United States
Spring Conference Coalition for Juvenile Justice
1993

❧7❧
A Call to Action

In response to the range of policy, program, and practice issues that impact on kinship care, CWLA proposes a national agenda aimed at institutionalizing and improving kinship care services. The agenda outlines roles for child welfare agencies in advancing the kinship care policy, program, and practice recommendations advanced in this report; directions for legislative action; and research that addresses kinship care issues.

An Agenda for Child Welfare Agencies

CWLA strongly urges child welfare agencies to immediately take steps to implement the recommendations contained in this report. CWLA encourages child welfare agencies to adopt the principles that guide the policy and practice framework for kinship care and to take action steps to implement the recommendations for (1) assessment of kin and approval and licensing of kinship parents; (2) the development of comprehensive services for children in kinship care, their birth parents and their kinship parents; (3) equitable and adequate financial support for children in kinship care; (4) preparation and support of kinship parents; (5) monitoring and supervision of kinship care homes; (6) permanency planning for children in kinship care through either reunification with parents, adoption by kin, guardianship, long-term kinship care, or nonrelative adoption; (7) staff training, support and recognition; and (8) information systems.

CWLA urges child welfare agencies to work together and with national, state, and local organizations to further address crosscutting kinship care policy and practice issues, including:

- the relationship between intergenerational programs, programs for the aging, and child welfare programs;

- the interstate placement of children;

- federal policy and regulations related to kinship care; and

- evaluation of kinship care programs.

Legislative Directions

A comprehensive legislative agenda for children and their families should be developed and advanced to support kinship care as an essential child welfare service. This agenda should include the following components:

- Expand provisions that acknowledge and, on a routine basis, include kinship care as an essential part of the array of child welfare services supported under current federal laws, including the Adoption Assistance and Child Welfare Act of 1980, as amended; the Child Abuse Prevention and Treatment Act; the Adoption Opportunities Act; the Juvenile Justice and Delinquency Prevention Act; the Alcohol, Drug Abuse and Mental Health Block Grants; the Abandoned Infants Assistance Act; and the various child day care federal/state programs.

- Improve and make more consistent the financial and

social supports to kin across federal and—to the extent possible—state programs so that children receiving kinship care in child welfare system are assured financial and other benefits similar to children in family foster care arrangements, and that children and kin families are not penalized because of their relationship. For children likely to remain with kin for a long period of time, efforts should include providing federal reimbursement to states for subsidized guardianship payments for children in kinship care under a program similar to subsidized special needs adoption and federal legislation to allow kinship parents to include children in their care on their health insurance plans.

- Build upon and utilize opportunities afforded by the recently enacted child welfare services legislation under the Omnibus Budget Reconciliation Act of 1993 to educate the field and policymakers at all levels about kinship care as a family preservation program. Also, ensure that implementation of the new child welfare services legislation involves activities (e.g., development of regulations, evaluation, training, and technical assistance) that include attention to kinship care issues.

As the federal government and the states continue moving toward major health care and welfare reform, each of these efforts will have significant implications for children, families, and caregivers involved in the delivery of child welfare services. Key questions have already emerged in the debate on health care reform concerning access and benefits for low-income and vulnerable children and families who comprise the bulk of the child welfare population. As is true for all vulnerable children, ensuring continuous and adequate health care coverage for children in kinship care will require particular attention.

Similarly, kinship care issues require special attention in any welfare reform initiative. Almost half of the children in foster care are AFDC-eligible. As noted earlier, public financial support for care by kin can come from several sources including AFDC, federal foster care, or state-funded foster care (with widely varying state benefit levels). As the welfare reform debate proceeds, it will be necessary to explore the incentives and disincentives of differing benefit structures as they impact on family preservation, family reunification, and out-of-home care. Attention also needs to be given to the possible effects of changing AFDC benefit levels or time-limiting benefits. These and other issues must be raised to ensure that reforms work in concert with the array of child welfare and related services to protect children, provide child and family supports as needed, and promote self-sufficiency.

A Research Agenda

CWLA calls on the U.S. Department of Health and Human Services to conduct a comprehensive study of kinship care. Areas for study should include, but not be limited to, the following:

- demographic information on children, birth parents, and kinship parents, including age, sex, race/ethnicity, income sources, and education;

- the service needs of children in kinship care, including the need for social services, health care, and education, as well as service history (i.e., number of placements, length of time in care, permanency goals and outcomes);

- the characteristics of parents whose children enter kinship care as well as the reasons for placement and the reasons for the selection of kinship care versus other out-of-home care options;

- information on kinship parents, including their

relationships to birth parents and to children; informal or formal status; and health status of the kinship parents;

- outcomes for children in kinship care in terms of their physical, emotional, and developmental wellbeing; and comparisons of outcomes between informal and formal kinship care and between kinship care and other forms of out-of-home care.

❊8❊

CONCLUSION

Kinship care is still evolving as a part of the child welfare service delivery system. Child welfare agencies may call on kinship families to provide short-term emergency care, long-term care, or a permanent family environment in which a child can grow to adulthood. Kinship care is an essential child welfare service option. It has the potential—when appropriate assessment, planning, regulation, and support is available—to provide children with care, protection, and nurturing within the context of their families when they cannot safely remain with their parents.

This report provides child welfare agencies with policy, program, and practice recommendations to maximize the healthy growth and development of children in kinship care. It is only a beginning, however. More work is needed to address specific kinship care policies, program issues, and practice. CWLA member agencies will play a critical role in further shaping and defining quality kinship care programs, using this report to facilitate ongoing discussion and support for kinship care.

❧ Appendices ❧

❧ Appendix A ❧
REFERENCES

American Public Welfare Association. *Voluntary Cooperative Information System: Characteristics of Children in Substitute and Adoptive Care, Based on FY 82 through FY 89 Data.* Washington, DC: APWA, 1993.

American Public Welfare Association. *VCIS Research Notes: U.S. Child Substitute Care Flow Data for FY 92 and Current Trends in the State Child Substitute Care Populations.* Washington, DC: APWA, 1993.

Benedict, Mary I., and White, Roger B. "Factors Associated with Foster Care Length of Stay." *Child Welfare* LXX, 1 (January–February 1991): 45–58.

Berrick, Jill; Barth, Richard; and Needle, Barbara. "A Comparison of Kinship Foster Homes and Family Foster Homes," in *Child Welfare Research Review,* edited by R.P. Barth, J.D. Berrick, and N. Gilbert. New York: Columbia University Press, 1993.

Burton, Linda M. "Black Grandparents Rearing Children of Drug-Addicted Parents: Stressors, Outcomes, and Social Service Needs." *The Gerontologist* 32, 6 (December 1992): 744–751.

Child Welfare League of America. *Winning with Diversity.* Washington, DC 1992 (unpublished).

Congressional Research Services. *"Kinship" Foster Care: An Emerging Federal Issue.* Washington, DC: U.S. Government Printing Office, 1993.

Dubowitz, Howard. *The Physical and Mental Health and Educational Status of Children Placed with Relatives: Final Report.* Baltimore, MD: University of Maryland School of Medicine, 1990.

Home of Relative License Report, February 1992. Springfield, IL: Department of Children and Family Services, Bureau of Quality Assurance, Program Monitoring Division, State of Illinois, 1992.

Maryland Department of Human Resources. *Services to Extended Families with Children, Monthly Report 1993.* Baltimore, MD (interdepartmental report).

National Black Child Development Institute. *Parental Drug Abuse and African American Children in Foster Care: Issues and Study Findings.* Washington, DC: NBCDI, 1991.

National Committee for the Prevention of Child Abuse. *Current Trends Reporting and Fatalities: The Results of the 1992 Annual Fifty State Survey.* Chicago, IL: NCPCA, 1993.

National Foster Parent Association. *National Foster Care Facts and Figures.* Houston, TX: NFPA, 1991.

Takas, Marianne. *Kinship Care and Family Preservation: A Guide for States in Legal and Policy Development.* Washington, DC: American Bar Association Center on Children and the Law, 1993.

Task Force on Permanency Planning for Foster Children, Inc. *Kinship Care: The Double-Edged Dilemma.* Rochester, NY: Task Force on Permanency Planning for Children, 1990.

Testa, Mark. "Conditions of Risk for Substitute Care." *Children and Youth Services Review* 14, 1/2 (1992):27–36.

Thorton, Jesse L. "An Investigation into the Nature of Kinship Foster Homes." D.S.W. dissertation, September, 1987.

Thorton, Jesse L. "Permanency Planning for Children in Kinship Foster Homes." *Child Welfare* LXX, 5 (September–October 1991): 593–601.

United State Bureau of Census. *Current Population Reports 1992.* Washington, DC: U.S. Government Printing Office, 1993.

United States Department of Health and Human Services, Inspector General. *Using Relatives for Foster Care and State Practices in Using Relatives for Foster Care.* Washington, DC: U.S. Government Printing Office, # OEI-06-90-02391 (companion volume), 1992.

U.S. House of Representatives Committee on Ways and Means. *Overview of Entitlement Programs: 1993 Green Book.* Washington, DC: U.S. Government Printing Office, 1993.

Wulczyn, Fred H., and Goerge, Robert M. *Foster Care in New York and Illinois: The Challenge of Rapid Change.* Chicago: Chapin Hall Center for Children, 1991.

❧ Appendix B ❧
The CWLA North American Kinship Care Policy and Practice Committee

Chairperson

Ivory L. Johnson, Deputy Director, Children Services, San Diego County Dept. of Social Services, San Diego, CA

Staff Directors

Dana Burdnell Wilson, MSW, Program Director, Kinship Care Service and Cultural Competence, CWLA, Washington, DC

Eileen Mayers Pasztor, DSW, Program Director, Family Foster Care and International Projects, CWLA, Washington, DC

Members

Joseph Altheimer, Executive Director, Institute for Families and Children, New York, NY

Lynn Biggs, Foster Home Developer, The Casey Family Program, Yakima, WA

Frank E. Boxwill, Consultant, Family Institute for More Effective Living, Inc., Pennsburg, PA

Carolyn Buck, Senior Director of Services, Children's Aid Society of Metro Toronto, Toronto, ON

Nancy Cavaluzzi, Executive Director, Louise Wise Services, New York, NY

T. Michael Decker, Director, San Bernardino County Department of Aging and Adult Services, San Bernardino, CA

Richard P. Dina, Executive Director, Children's House, Inc., Mineola, NY

Jean Doll, Administrator, Foster Care Program, Children and Family Services Division, North Dakota Dept. of Human Services, Bismarck, ND

Howard Dubowitz, MD, Department of Pediatrics, University of Maryland School of Medicine, Baltimore, MD

Karl Ensign, Program Analyst, U.S. Department of Health and Human Services, Humphrey Building Room 404E, Washington, DC

Ramona L. Foley, Director of Substitute Care, South Carolina Department of Social Services, Columbia, SC

Judith Gallo, Assistant Commissioner for Bureau of Program Planning, New York State Department of Social Services, Albany, NY

Charlotte Goodluck, Assistant Professor, Social Work Program, Northern Arizona University, Flagstaff, AZ

Robert B. Hill, Director, Institute for Urban Research, Morgan State University, Baltimore, MD

Sondra M. Jackson, Director, Training Department, School of Social Work and Community Planning, University of Maryland, Baltimore, MD

Beverly W. Jones, Assistant Professor, University of Maryland School of Social Work, Baltimore, MD

James C. Jones, Deputy Director, Central Baptist Children's Home, Chicago, IL

David Kirk, President/Chief Executive Officer, ChildServ, Chicago, IL

Carl W. Koerner, Executive Director, Family Care Services of Metropolitan Chicago, Chicago, IL

Deborah Langosch, Clinical Social Worker, Bensonhurst Guidance Center, Brooklyn, NY

Maryjane Link, Adoption Specialist, New York State Department of Social Services, Buffalo, NY

Robert L. Little, Commissioner, Child Welfare Administration, New York, NY

Megan McLaughlin, Executive Director and Chief Executive Officer, Federation of Protestant Welfare Agencies, New York, NY

Elba Montalvo, Executive Director, Commission for Hispanic Children and Families, Inc., New York, NY

Beatrice Moore, Child Welfare Specialist, U.S. Children's Bureau, Washington, DC,

Alex Morales, Associate Executive Director, Children's Bureau of Southern California, Los Angeles, CA

Donna Petras , Chief, Office of Foster Care, Illinois Department of Children & Family Services, Chicago, IL

Eileen Nagel Rafield, Associate Executive Director, Jewish Child Care Association, New York, NY

Patricia Reynolds, Program Officer, Stuart Foundations, San Francisco, CA

Gerri Robinson, Program Manager for Resource Recruitment, Maryland Department of Human Resources, Baltimore, MD

Carolyne B. Rodriguez, Division Director, The Casey Family Program—Austin Division, Austin, TX

Betsey Rosenbaum, Director, National Commission on Child Welfare and Family Preservation Project, American Public Welfare Association, Washington, DC

Deborah Shore, Executive Director, Sasha Bruce Youthwork, Inc., Washington, DC

Mark D. Simms, MD, American Academy of Pediatrics, Committee on Early Childhood Adoption and Dependent Care, St. Mary's Hospital—PAC, Waterbury, CT

Gene L. Svebakken, Executive Director, Lutheran Child & Family Services of Illinois, River Forest, IL

Marianne Takas, Assistant Staff Director, American Bar Association—Center on Children and Law, Washington, DC

Janet Thaxton, Senior Director of Programs, Boston Children's Services, Boston, MA

Donna Walgren, Executive Director, Children and Families of Iowa, Des Moines, IA

Clarice Dibble Walker, Commissioner, District of Columbia Department of Human Services, Commission on Social Services, Washington, DC

Doris A. Walker, Chief of Foster Care Unit, Georgia Division of Family and Children Services, Atlanta, GA

Cora E. White, President, National Foster Parent Association, Madison, WI

Ex-Officio

John Mattingly, Senior Associate, The Annie E. Casey Foundation, Greenwich, CT

Marsha Rose Wickliffe, Program Associate, The Annie E. Casey Foundation, Greenwich, CT

Wendell Primus, Staff Director, Subcommittee on Human Resources, House Ways and Means Committee, U.S. House of Representatives, Washington, DC

Consultants

Jill Duerr Berrick, Director, Child Welfare Research Center, University of California at Berkeley, Berkeley, CA

Ethel Dunn, Executive Director, Grandparents United For Children's Rights, National Headquarters/Data Center, Madison, WI

Emily Jean McFadden, Professor, School of Social Work, and National Foster Care Resource Center for Family, Group, and Residential Care, Eastern Michigan University, Ypsilanti, MI

Mary Onama, Director, Foster Care, Kinship and Adoption, Edwin Gould Services for Children, New York, NY

Annette Samuels, Director, D.C. Commission for Women, Kinship Care Coalition, Washington, DC

Sylvie de Toledo, President, Grandparents as Parents, Culver City, CA